Take a trip to
ARGENTINA

Keith Lye

General Editor

Henry Pluckrose

Franklin Watts

London   New York   Sydney   Toronto

Facts about Argentina

Area:
2,766,889 sq. km.
(1,068,302 sq. miles)

Population:
28,773,000

Capital:
Buenos Aires

Largest cities:
Buenos Aires (2,908,000)
Córdoba (969,000)
Rosario (935,000)

Official language:
Spanish

Religion:
Christianity

Main exports:
Farm products, including
hides and skins, maize,
meat, vegetable oils,
wheat and wool

Currency:
Austral

Franklin Watts Limited
12a Golden Square
London W1

ISBN: UK Edition 0 86 313 442 4
ISBN: US Edition 0 531 10194 0
Library of Congress Catalog
Card No: 86 50017

© Franklin Watts Limited 1986

Typeset by Ace Filmsetting Ltd,
Frome, Somerset
Printed in Hong Kong

Maps: Tony Payne

Design: Edward Kinsey

Stamps: Stanley Gibbons Limited

Photographs: Zefa, 12, 21, 24, 26, 29;
Tony & Marion Morrison, 3, 4, 5, 6, 7,
10, 13, 14, 15, 16, 18, 20, 22, 23, 25, 27,
28, 30, 31; Paul Forrester 8; Travel
Photo International, 17; Robert
Harding, 19
Front cover: Zefa
Back cover: Tony & Marion Morrison

Argentina is South America's second largest country. The Andes Mountains, including Aconcagua, the highest peak in the Americas at 6,959 m (22,831 ft), run along the border with Chile in the west. Argentina's name comes from a Latin word, argentum, or silver, which Spanish explorers hoped to find there.

East of the Andes is a hilly region. Large areas are desert, where the few plants, such as cacti, must withstand long droughts. Mountain streams flow through many valleys. Their water is used to irrigate farmland.

4

A large region in the north is called the Gran Chaco. This region has mild, dry winters and warm, wet summers. There are large forests and grassy plains, but only a few people live there.

The central plains of Argentina, the pampas, are fertile. These plains cover about a fourth of the country. They are the home of two out of every three Argentinians. The pampas have a mild climate. Cereal farms are in the east and ranches in the drier west.

The world's southernmost town, Ushuaia, is on the island of Tierra del Fuego, which Argentina shares with Chile. Southern Argentina is a cold region. It consists mostly of a dry, windswept plateau called Patagonia. It is thinly populated.

The picture shows some stamps
and money used in Argentina. The
main unit of currency, the austral,
has replaced the original peso. The
austral contains 100 centavos.

WORLD
MAP

Argentina

BOLIVIA

Salta

Gran Chaco

PARAGUAY

San Miguel
de Tucuman

Resistencia

▲ *Iguaçu
Falls*

A
N
D
E
S

BRAZIL

Córdoba

Santa Fé

Mt Aconcagua
6959 ▲

Rosario

Mendoza

URUGUAY

Buenos Aires

La Plata

PACIFIC
OCEAN

C
H
I
L
E

A
N
D
E
S

M
O
U
N
T
A
I
N
S

ARGENTINA

Mar del Plata

Bahia Blanca

ATLANTIC
OCEAN

P
A
T
A
G
O
N
I
A

Comodoro Rivadavia

Falkland Is.

Tierra del Fuego

Ushuaia

9

Spain ruled Argentina from the 16th century. Argentina declared itself independent on July 9, 1816. The leader of the independence struggle was General José de San Martín, whose statue is shown here in the northeastern town of Concordia.

Most Argentinians are descendants of Spanish and Italian settlers. Argentina also has a few Indians and some people of mixed European and Indian descent. The picture shows Córdoba, Argentina's second largest city. It was founded in 1573.

Argentina's capital and largest city, Buenos Aires, is the chief port. It has many industries. The picture shows the Avenida 9 de Julio (the 9th of July Avenue), named after Argentina's independence day. About 84 out of every 100 Argentinians live in cities and towns.

Congress Hall in Buenos Aires
houses the parliament. It consists of
a 254-member House of Deputies
and a 46-member Senate. Argentina
is a republic and an elected President
is Head of State. In 1976, a military
government took power. But civilian
rule was restored in December 1983.

Salta, a city in the beautiful northwest of Argentina, was founded in 1582. It has several old buildings, including its Cathedral, which was built between 1858 and 1878. The Cathedral stands on Salta's central square, the Plaza 9 de Julio.

Salta's Cathedral contains many valuable objects, including a gold altar. Nine out of every ten Argentinians are Roman Catholics. There are also about 500,000 Protestants and 300,000 Jews.

15

About 13 out of every 100 workers
are employed in farming. Argentina
is the world's third most important
beef producing country after the USA
and Russia. The cowboys in this
picture are called gauchos.

16

Pasture for animals covers about two fifths of Argentina. Sheep are reared in Patagonia and the drier parts of the pampas. Argentina is one of the world's leading wool producers. Much of the wool is exported to the USA.

About a tenth of Argentina's land is cultivated. Wheat, the chief crop, grows on the pampas. Other crops are citrus fruits, cotton, maize, soya beans and sugar cane. Grapes are grown to make wine. Argentina is the world's fifth largest wine producer.

Oil is Argentina's leading resource. Oil and natural gas are mined in Patagonia and in the foothills of the Andes Mountains. The oilfield shown here is at Comodoro Rivadavia, in Patagonia. Argentina produces nearly all the oil and natural gas it needs.

Nearly two fifths of Argentina's electricity supply comes from hydro-electric power stations. This dam is on the Uruguay River, which forms part of Argentina's border with Uruguay and Brazil.

About 28 out of every 100 workers in Argentina are employed in industry. Leading products are steel, shown here, cars, cement and chemicals. Argentina is a fast developing country. Experts think that it will become a leading industrial power in the next century.

About 93 per cent of adults in Argentina can read and write. Education for children from 6 to 14 is now free and compulsory. But a much smaller percentage of children obtain higher education.

Argentina has about 40 universities. The oldest university, shown here, is in Córdoba. It was founded in 1613. The largest university is in Buenos Aires. There are more than half a million university students in Argentina.

Meat, especially beef, is a popular food. Here, a barbecue is being prepared by two gauchos. One of them is drinking wine from a skin bag. But the national drink is maté, a tea made from the leaves of a holly tree.

Soccer is Argentina's leading sport. The national team won the World Cup in 1978. Winter sports in the mountains, basketball, boating, golf, polo and car and horse racing are other popular activities.

Mar del Plata is a famous seaside resort. It is in central Argentina. About two million people go there every year, many of whom are wealthy families from Buenos Aires, which is 400 km (250 miles) to the north.

Workers enjoy sunbathing in the many parks in Buenos Aires. City people are wealthier than farmers. In recent years, many farm workers have gone to live in the cities. Those who cannot find jobs may be forced to live in slums.

The Iguaçu Falls on the border between Argentina and Brazil are one of South America's most famous tourist attractions. Iguaçu is an Indian word meaning great waters. About a million tourists visit Argentina every year.

The beautiful Lake Nahuel Huapi is in a national park on the border with Chile. Visitors can take trips on the lake and enjoy the scenery of this area, which is often called the Switzerland of South America.

The Falkland Islands are a British colony, lying about 480 km (300 miles) east of southern Argentina. The only important town is Stanley. Argentina claims the Falkland Islands as its property. These islands are called the Islas Malvinas in Argentina.

In April 1982, Argentina's armed
forces seized the Falkland Islands.
But Britain sent ships and soldiers to
the islands and regained them in
June. The main activity of the
Falkland islanders is sheep rearing.
Wool is the main product.

Index